MY FIRST STEPS
Baby Boy

Photographs by Elle Mendenhall

vmb
PUBLISHERS

Contents

Here I am!

The birth

Name

_____

Day of the week

_____

Date

_____

Time

_____

Weight

_____

Length

_____

Where it happened

_____

Medical team/ doctor and midwife

_____

First impressions and reactions

Mummy's first words

_____

_____

_____

Daddy's first words

_____

_____

_____

Reactions of family and friends

_____

_____

_____

Hopes for the baby

_____

_____

_____

Photographs

M

Precious memories

Hospital wrist tag

The lock of hair

The first visits

The first gifts

Well wishers' cards

Personal details

	at birth	at 6 months	at 1 year
Color of eyes			
Color of hair			
Complexion			
Distinguishing features			

Star
Sign

My name

My name was chosen by

_____

_____

It was chosen because

_____

_____

My nickname is

_____

_____

What was going on in the world

Newspaper headlines on the day I was born

The hit songs

The popular films

The book of the year

World leaders at the time

Some current prices at the time (1 liter of milk)

My family

great grandfather

great grandfather

great grandmother

great grandmother

grandmother

grandfather

uncles/aunts

mummy

sisters

me

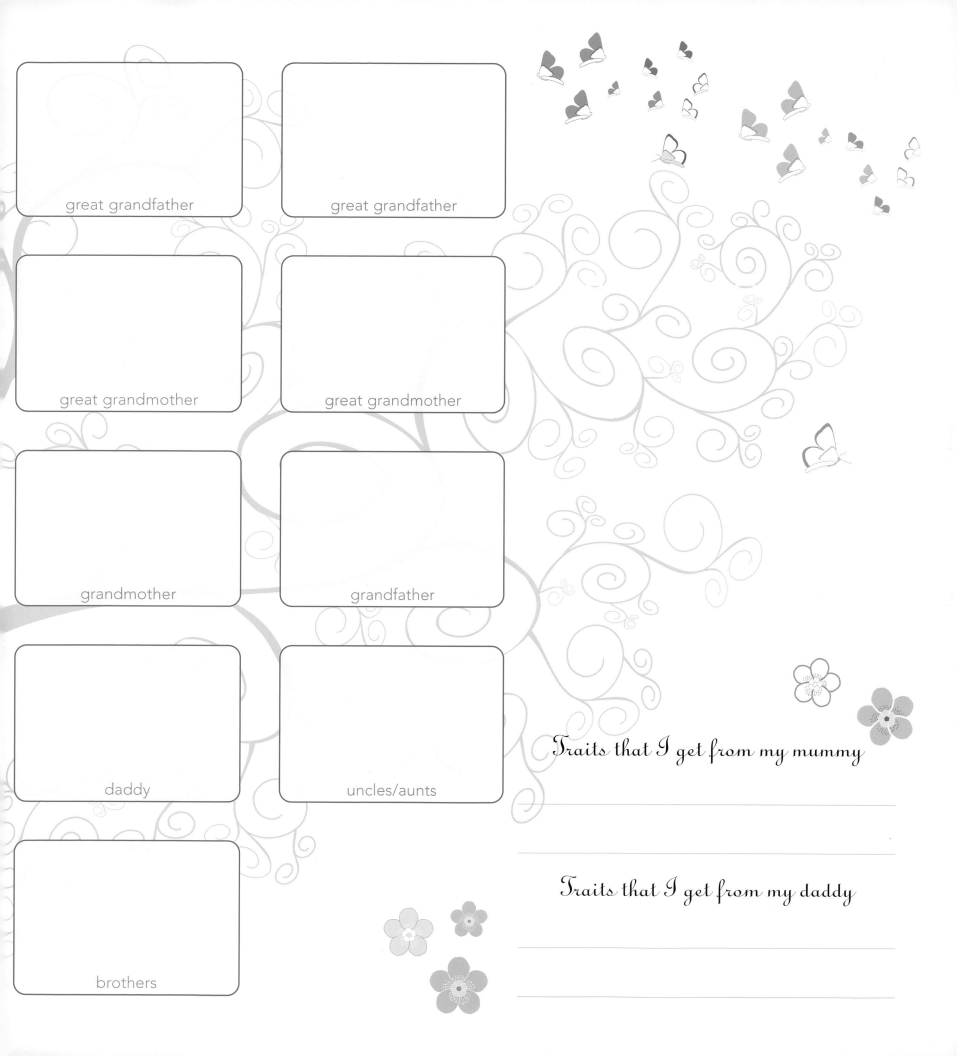

great grandfather

great grandfather

great grandmother

great grandmother

grandmother

grandfather

daddy

uncles/aunts

brothers

Traits that I get from my mummy

Traits that I get from my daddy

Photographs

Coming home

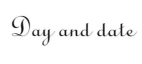

Day and date

_____

Weather conditions

_____

What the baby was wearing

_____

Who brought the baby home

_____

First address

_____

_____

How the room was decorated

_____

_____

_____

Photographs

Medical records

Blood group

_____

Medical examinations

Date	Doctor	In relation to

Vaccinations

_____

_____

Allergies

_____

_____

Weight and height table

	weight	height
At birth		
One month		
Two months		
Three months		
Four months		
Five months		
Six months		
Nine months		
Twelve months		
Eighteen months		
Two years		
Three years		

Dental card

central incisor | central incisor

lateral incisor | lateral incisor

canine | canine

first molar | first molar

second molar | second molar

jaw

left side | right side

second molar | jaw | second molar

first molar | first molar

canine | canine

lateral incisor | lateral incisor

central incisor | central incisor

How was the first tooth spotted and by whom

Comments on the first dental examination

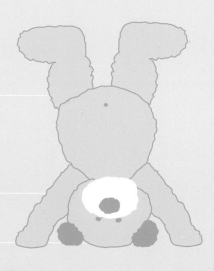

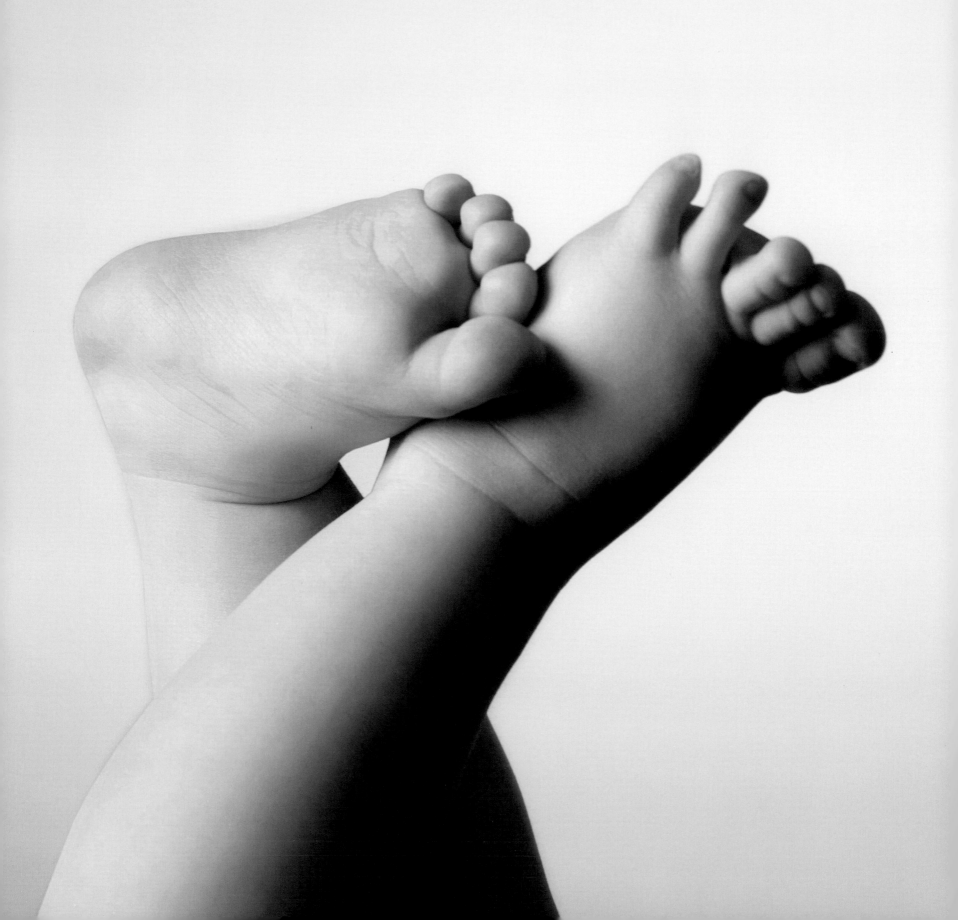

Foot print

Hand print

My day

Bath time

Baby's reactions

_____

_____

_____

Favorite toys

_____

_____

_____

Water games

_____

_____

_____

Photographs

Photographs

F  Baby food

First time I ate solid food

First time I held a spoon

First time I drank out of a cup

Food I liked

Food I did not like

Sleep

Bedtime rituals

_____

_____

_____

My cutest sleeping habit

_____

_____

_____

Important dates

first night in a cot _____

first night in a bed _____

My favorite lullabies

_____

_____

_____

Sleep, baby, sleep,
Thy papa guards the sheep;
Thy mama shakes the dreamland tree
And from it fall sweet dreams for thee,
Sleep, baby, sleep,
Our cottage vale is deep;
The little lambie is on the green,
With woolly fleece so soft and clean,
Sleep, baby, sleep,
Down where the woodbines creep;
Be always like the lamb so mild,
A kind and sweet and gentle child,
Sleep, baby sleep.

Sleepyhead, close your eyes.

Mother's right here beside you.

I'll protect you from harm,

You will wake in my arms.

Guardian angels are near,

So sleep on, with no fear.

Beautiful dreamer, wake unto me,

Starlight and dewdrops are waiting for thee;

Sounds of the rude world, heard in the day,

Lull'd by the moonlight have all pass'd away!

Beautiful dreamer, awake unto me!

Beautiful dreamer, awake unto me!

My first outings

First time I walked

_____

Place

_____

Day

_____

Baby's reaction

_____

First car trip

_____

Reactions

_____

First train journey/flight

_____

Reactions

_____

Photographs

The first time to ...

The first time to recognize mummy and daddy

The first time to lift head and shoulders

The first time to follow a moving object with eyes

The first time to play with feet

The first time to hold a toy

The first time to point at something

The first animal noises

The first drawing

M Learning to move

Moving on all fours/crawling

Standing up alone

Walking with help

Walking alone

Going up stairs

Running

Jumping

Loves dancing

Photographs

Laughter and tears

The first smile

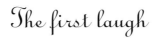

The first laugh

Things that made me happy

The things that frightened me

The things that comforted me

Games

Favorite games

_____

_____

Favorite games with mummy

_____

_____

Favorite games with daddy

_____

_____

Play mates

_____

_____

Favorite activities with friends

_____

_____

Favorite things

Toys

Places

Clothes

Books

Activities

Songs

Colors

Fairytale characters

The baby's day
at one month

Sleeping times
_____

_____

Feeding times
_____

_____

Play time
_____

_____

Mummy's memories
_____

_____

at three months

Sleeping times
_____

_____

Feeding times
_____

_____

Play time
_____

_____

Mummy's memories
_____

_____

at six months

Sleeping times

Feeding times

Play time

Mummy's memories

at twelve months

Sleeping times

Feeding times

Play time

Mummy's memories

at two years

Mummy's memories

at three years

Mummy's memories

H Going on holiday

My first holiday

The time of year

Baby's age

Other people on holiday with us

What we did

Baby's reactions

Photographs

Ceremonies and special occasions

Event

_____

Date

_____

Relations and friends present

_____

_____

_____

_____

Important events to remember

_____

_____

_____

_____

Photographs

*B*First birthday

How we celebrated

_____

_____

Who was there

_____

_____

_____

The birthday cake

_____

The baby's reactions

_____

_____

My favorite present

_____

Photographs

Second birthday

Things to remember ...

_____

_____

_____

_____

B Third birthday

Things to remember ...

_____

_____

_____

_____

Useful telephone numbers

Editorial Coordination
Giada Francia

Graphic Design
Marinella Debernardi

Drawings
Clara Zanotti

Elle Mendenhall, founder of Ella Bella Photography, with headquarters
in Austin (Texas), is specialized in creative portraits of newborn babies and children, in natural light.
Elle is one of the leading Texan portrait photographers and is much appreciated for her style
and her modern approach to photography.

Photo credits
All photographs are by Elle Mendenhall (Ella Bella Photography) except the following:
page 44 - Edvard March/Corbis; page 47 - moodboard/Corbis; page 75 - Morgan David de Lossy/Corbis;
page 81 - Getty Images; page 88 - Rebecca Emery/Getty Images

VMB Publishers® is a registered trademark property of Edizioni White Star s.r.l.

© 2010 Edizioni White Star s.r.l.
Via Candido Sassone, 24 - 13100 Vercelli, Italy
www.whitestar.it

Translation: Catherine Howard

ISBN 978-88-540-1536-4
1 2 3 4 5 6   14 13 12 11 10

Printed in Thailand

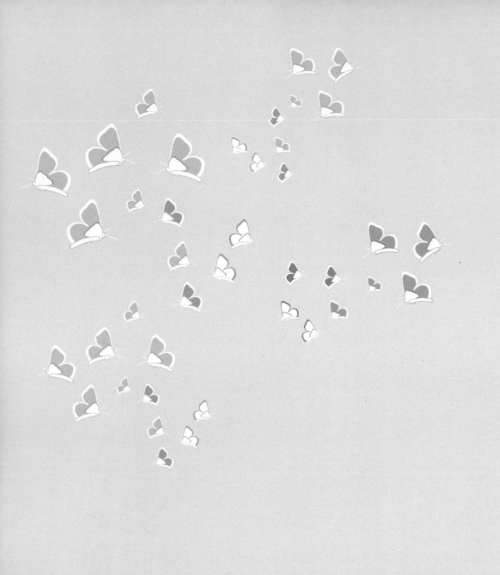